The Ultimate Ome Cookbook

Healthy, Tasty Omelette Recipes Easy to Prepare and Share!

by Olivia Rana

Olivia Rana © 2024

License Notes

No part of this Book, either for personal use, commercial use, should be reproduced or distributed without full written permission from the author. This is prohibited by the law.

Also, this book is strictly meant to entertain you. As such, the reader is liable for any damages that the book or its content causes.

Table of Contents

Introduction 5

Delicious Omelette Recipe Collection 6

    1. Mushrooms & Onions Omelette 7

    2. Thai Omelette 9

    3. Cheddar & Broccoli Omelette 11

    4. Sausage & Apple Omelette 13

    5. Potato & Leek Omelette 15

    6. Steak & Cheese Omelette 17

    7. Cheese & Zucchini Omelette 19

    8. Roasted Red Pepper & Onion Omelette 21

    9. Cheddar & Kale Omelette 23

    10. Pepper Jack Cheese & Salsa Omelette 25

    11. Turkey & Ham Omelette 27

    12. Tomato & Spinach Omelette 29

    13. Roasted Butternut Squash Omelette 31

    14. Cheese & Pepper Omelette 34

15. Swiss Cheese & Bacon Omelette 36

16. Greek Omelette 38

17. Ham & Cheese Omelette 40

18. Mexican Omelette 42

19. Brie & Herb Omelette 44

20. Crab Omelette 46

21. Western Omelette 48

22. Smoked Salmon & Green Onion Omelette 50

23. Four Cheese Omelette 52

24. Spanish Omelette 54

25. Artichoke & Goat Cheese Omelette 56

26. White Cheddar & Apple Smoked Bacon Omelette 58

27. Pizza Omelette 60

28. Mediterranean Omelette 62

29. Shrimp Omelette 64

30. Indian Omelette 66

Conclusion 68

Afterword 69

Introduction

Within these pages, you are about to discover a wonderful array of omelette recipes that you will not only find flavourful but easy to prepare! An omelette is a great dish that can be served for any meal. It is a healthy choice of meals to prepare; especially on days when your time is limited. You can whip up a tasty omelette in literally minutes! If you are trying to introduce your children to learn how to prepare a meal-making an omelette is a good way to help get them to prepare their own cuisine. Encourage them to try adding new ingredients to the base omelet ingredients. There is nothing like enjoying a meal that you have prepared and created on your own! Now it is time to get your omelet of choice whipped up!

Delicious Omelette Recipe Collection

1. Mushrooms & Onions Omelette

A great way to start your day is to sit down and enjoy this yummy omelette!

Prep time: 5 minutes

Cook time: 16 minutes

Servings: 1

Ingredients:

- 1 cup of button mushrooms, sliced
- 3 large eggs
- 2 tablespoons milk
- 1 small onion, diced
- ½ cup Swiss cheese, shredded
- 1 teaspoon olive oil
- sea salt (fine) & ground black pepper to taste

Directions:

1. In a nonstick skillet over medium heat, warm the oil. Add the mushrooms and onion to the pan and sauté for about 6 minutes. Remove from the skillet and set aside.
2. In a mixing bowl, whisk the eggs with milk, salt and pepper.
3. Add egg mixture to the pan and cook for a few minutes until it starts to set. Add the mushrooms mixture to the pan and top with cheese.
4. Continue to cook for another few minutes or until the egg is set, then flip half the omelette over and cook for another minute. Slide onto a serving plate and enjoy!

2. Thai Omelette

Enjoy this wonderful exotic flavourful omelette that is sure to please!

Prep time: 8 minutes

Cook time: 7 minutes

Servings: 1

Ingredients:

- 2 tablespoons milk
- 3 large eggs
- 1 scallion, chopped
- 1 teaspoon fresh lime juice
- 1 teaspoon fish sauce
- 2 teaspoons white pepper powder
- 1 teaspoon olive oil
- ¼ cup sausage, cooked & chopped
- handful of cilantro, chopped
- sea salt (fine) & ground black pepper to taste

Directions:

1. In a skillet placed over medium heat, warm the oil.
2. In a bowl, whisk the eggs, fish sauce, milk and white pepper.
3. Add the remaining ingredients and continue whisking eggs until frothy.
4. Pour the mixture into a skillet and cook for a few minutes or until the eggs have set.
5. Flip the omelette over using two spatulas on either side. Brown for 2 minutes. Serve and enjoy!

3. Cheddar & Broccoli Omelette

A yummy-tasting omelette that can easily be whipped up in minutes!

Prep time: 5 minutes

Cook time: 7 minutes

Servings: 1

Ingredients:

- ½ cup broccoli, cooked
- 3 large eggs
- ½ cup sharp cheddar cheese, shredded
- 2 tablespoons milk
- 1 teaspoon olive oil
- sea salt (fine) & ground black pepper to taste

Directions:

1. Heat your oil in a nonstick skillet over medium heat.
2. In a mixing bowl, whisk eggs, milk, salt and pepper.
3. Add the egg mixture to the skillet and cook until starting to set, then add broccoli on one side of the omelette.
4. Sprinkle with cheese over the entire omelette. Cook until eggs have set and cheese is melted.
5. Flip half of the omelette without broccoli over and continue to cook for another 2 minutes. Serve and enjoy!

4. Sausage & Apple Omelette

Enjoy this delectable omelette that makes for a perfect lunch meal!

Prep time: 5 minutes

Cook time: 8 minutes

Servings: 1

Ingredients:

- 1 hot Italian sausage, casing removed
- 2 tablespoons milk
- 3 large eggs
- 2 tablespoons butter
- 1 scallion, chopped
- 1 small Granny Smith apple, cored & finely chopped
- ½ cup cheddar cheese, shredded
- 1 tablespoon olive oil
- sea salt (fine) & black pepper to taste

Directions:

1. Heat the oil in a nonstick skillet over medium-high heat. Add the sausage and cook for about 3 minutes.
2. Add the scallion and apple and stir in until the sausage is browned or for about 4 minutes.
3. Remove skillet from heat and set aside.
4. In another pan, melt the butter over medium heat. Whisk the eggs with milk, salt and pepper. Add eggs to pan for 3 minutes or until starting to set. Add sausage mixture and top with cheese. Once cheese has melted, flip half over and cook for another 2 minutes. Serve and enjoy!

5. Potato & Leek Omelette

A tasty and filling omelette that is perfect to serve along with a salad of your choice!

Prep time: 10 minutes

Cook time: 35 minutes

Servings: 3

Ingredients:

- 2 large potatoes, peeled & thinly sliced
- 8 large eggs
- ½ cup leeks, thinly sliced
- 1 teaspoon olive oil
- 3 tablespoons parsley, chopped
- 1 white onion, peeled & sliced
- sea salt (fine) & ground black pepper to taste

Directions:

1. Heat oil in a nonstick skillet over medium heat. Add the onions, and leaks and sauté for about 5 minutes. Add the potatoes and cook covered for about 30 minutes, while stirring occasionally.

2. Whisk the eggs and season with salt and pepper. Stir in the parsley and add the egg mixture to the pan for a few minutes.

3. Once cooked, invert the omelette onto a plate, then serve and enjoy!

6. Steak & Cheese Omelette

Savour this yummy omelette for a hearty breakfast, lunch or dinner meal!

Prep time: 10 minutes

Cook time: 15 minutes

Servings: 1

Ingredients:

- ¼ cup green bell pepper, finely chopped
- 3 large eggs
- 2 tablespoons milk
- ¼ cup red onion, diced
- 2 tablespoons butter
- ¼ cup cooked steak, thinly sliced
- ½ cup cheddar cheese, shredded
- sea salt (fine) & ground black pepper to taste

Directions:

1. Melt your butter in a nonstick skillet over medium heat. Add the bell pepper and onion, then sauté for 5 minutes.
2. Add the sliced steak and cook for another minute. Remove the mixture from the pan and set aside.
3. Whisk eggs in a bowl with milk, salt and pepper. Add the eggs to the pan and cook until set, then add the steak mixture. Sprinkle with cheese evenly.
4. Cook until the cheese has melted, flip the omelette over and cook for another minute. Serve and enjoy!

7. Cheese & Zucchini Omelette

A tasty omelette that is full of healthy vegetables!

Prep time: 8 minutes

Cook time: 7 minutes

Servings: 1

Ingredients:

- 2 tablespoons milk
- 3 large eggs
- ½ cup zucchini, sliced
- ¼ cup grape tomatoes, quartered
- ¼ cup red onion, diced
- ½ cup Fontina cheese, shredded
- 1 tablespoon olive oil
- sea salt (fine) & ground black pepper to taste

Directions:

1. In a nonstick skillet, heat oil over medium heat. Add the onion and zucchini and sauté until soft for about 5 minutes. Add the tomatoes and cook for another minute or so.
2. In a mixing bowl, combine or whisk eggs, milk, salt and pepper together.
3. Add eggs to pan and cook until egg mixture begins to set, then add in shredded cheese.
4. Cook until the egg mixture is set, flip half the omelette over and cook for another minute. Serve immediately and enjoy!

8. Roasted Red Pepper & Onion Omelette

Enjoy the deep smoky flavour of roasted red peppers in this omelette!

Prep time: 8 minutes

Cook time: 8 minutes

Servings: 1

Ingredients:

- 1 cup cheddar cheese, shredded
- 3 large eggs
- 2 tablespoons milk
- half of a red pepper
- 1 teaspoon olive oil
- sea salt (fine) & fresh ground black pepper

Directions:

1. Using tongs roast red pepper over the flame of the stovetop until all of the outer skin is blackened.
2. After cooking, peel off the skin and chop into small pieces.
3. In a nonstick skillet, heat the oil over medium heat. Add the onion and sauté until softened.
4. In a mixing bowl, combine or whisk eggs, milk, salt and pepper. Add eggs to the pan and cook until starting to set. Add in the cheese and bell peppers.
5. Continue to cook until eggs are set, then flip half of the omelette to continue to cook for another minute. Serve and enjoy!

9. Cheddar & Kale Omelette

You can enjoy this yummy omelette with only a few simple ingredients!

Prep time: 8 minutes

Cook time: 8 minutes

Servings: 1

Ingredients:

- 2 tablespoons milk
- 3 large eggs
- 1 teaspoon olive oil
- 1 cup cheddar cheese, shredded
- ¼ cup red onion, diced
- 1 ½ cups kale leafs, chopped
- sea salt (fine) & fresh ground black pepper

Directions:

1. Heat the oil in a nonstick skillet over medium heat. Add in your onion along with kale then sauté for about 5 minutes. Remove pan from heat and set aside.
2. In a mixing bowl, whisk eggs, milk, salt and pepper. Add the egg mixture to the pan and cook until it starts to set. Add in the kale mixture and top with cheese.
3. Continue to cook until eggs are set, then flip one side of the omelette. Serve and enjoy!

10. Pepper Jack Cheese & Salsa Omelette

A flavourful and colourful omelette with peppers, cheese and salsa!

Prep time: 10 minutes

Cook time: 8 minutes

Servings: 1

Ingredients:

- 1 cup Pepper Jack cheese, shredded
- 3 large eggs
- 2 tablespoons butter
- 2 tablespoons milk
- ½ cup salsa, drained
- ½ cup green bell pepper, chopped
- sea salt (fine) & fresh ground black pepper to taste

Directions:

1. In a nonstick skillet over medium heat melt the butter. Add the bell pepper and onion, then sauté for about 5 minutes.
2. In a mixing bowl, whisk eggs, milk, salt and pepper. Add the egg mixture to the pan and cook until set. Spoon the salsa over the omelette and sprinkle with cheese.
3. Continue to cook until eggs are set, then flip over one half of the omelette and cook for another minute. Serve and enjoy!

11. Turkey & Ham Omelette

A great way to use up leftover turkey is to prepare this yummy omelette!

Prep time: 6 minutes

Cook time: 10 minutes

Servings: 1

Ingredients:

- 2 tablespoons of milk
- 3 large eggs
- 1 cup Swiss cheese, shredded
- 1 thick slice of cooked ham, chopped
- ¼ cup cooked turkey, shredded
- sea salt (fine) & ground black pepper to taste
- 1 teaspoon olive oil

Directions:

1. Heat your oil in a skillet placed over medium heat.
2. In a mixing bowl, whisk your eggs, milk, salt and pepper. Add the egg mixture to the skillet and cook for a few minutes until starting to set, then add in meats and top with cheese.
3. Cook undisturbed until the egg is set and the cheese is melted, then flip half of the omelette and cook for a few minutes until set. Serve and enjoy!

12. Tomato & Spinach Omelette

A hearty omelette recipe that makes for a filling meal!

Prep time: 5 minutes

Cook time: 8 minutes

Servings: 1

Ingredients:

- 2 tablespoons of milk
- 3 large eggs
- 1 cup Cheddar cheese, shredded
- 1 ½ cups baby spinach leafs, chopped
- 1 cup grape tomatoes, quartered
- ¼ cup red onion, finely diced
- sea salt (fine) & ground black pepper to taste
- 1 teaspoon olive oil

Directions:

1. Heat your oil in a nonstick skillet over medium heat.
2. Add the spinach and onion and sauté until the spinach is wilted and the onion is soft.
3. Add the tomatoes and cook for another minute, then remove from the pan and set aside.
4. In a mixing bowl, whisk your eggs, milk, salt and pepper together. Add the egg mixture to the pan and cook until starting to set, then add in the spinach mixture and top with cheese.
5. Cook until the cheese has melted and the egg is set, then flip half of the omelette over and cook for another minute. Serve and enjoy!

13. Roasted Butternut Squash Omelette

A bit more work is required to make this omelette but it will be well worth it!

Prep time: 20 minutes

Cook time: 55 minutes

Servings: 1

Ingredients:

- ½ a butternut squash
- 3 large eggs
- 2 tablespoons milk
- ¼ cup goat cheese
- 1 small onion, diced
- 1 clove garlic, minced
- 1 tablespoon butter
- 1 tablespoon olive oil
- sea salt (fine) & ground black pepper as needed

Directions:

1. Preheat your oven to 400° Fahrenheit. Peel and seed your butternut squash. Cut it into 1-inch cubes.

2. In a mixing bowl, toss your butternut squash with the olive oil. Season with salt and pepper and place on a baking sheet. Roast in your oven for 25 minutes or until the squash is tender.

3. Melt the butter in a nonstick skillet over medium heat. Add in the onion and caramelize for about 20 minutes. Add in the roasted butternut squash and garlic and continue to cook for another minute.

4. In a mixing bowl, whisk your eggs, milk, salt and pepper. Add your egg mixture to the skillet and cook until starting to set, then crumble in your goat's cheese.

5. Continue to cook the omelette until the egg is set, then flip half of your omelette over and cook for another minute. Serve and enjoy!

14. Cheese & Pepper Omelette

A yummy omelette that not only tastes great but looks amazing too!

Prep time: 10 minutes

Cook time: 8 minutes

Servings: 1

Ingredients:

- ¼ cup red onion, finely diced
- 3 large eggs
- 2 tablespoons of milk
- ¼ cup green bell pepper, diced
- 1 cup sharp cheddar cheese, shredded
- ¼ cup red bell pepper, diced
- 2 tablespoons butter
- sea salt (fine) & ground black pepper to taste

Directions:

1. Melt your butter in a nonstick skillet over medium heat. Add in bell pepper and onion then sauté for about 5 minutes.

2. In a mixing bowl, whisk your eggs, milk, salt and pepper. Add the egg mixture to the skillet and cook until starting to set, then add the cheese on top.

3. Cook until the cheese is melted, flip half of the omelette over and cook for another minute. Serve and enjoy!

15. Swiss Cheese & Bacon Omelette

An omelette recipe that has few ingredients but is full of spectacular flavour!

Prep time: 10 minutes

Cook time: 8 minutes

Servings: 1

Ingredients:

- 2 slices of bacon, cooked & crumbled
- 3 large eggs
- 2 tablespoons of milk
- 1 cup Swiss cheese, shredded
- 1 teaspoon olive oil
- sea salt (fine) & ground black pepper to taste

Directions:

1. Heat your oil in a nonstick skillet over medium heat.
2. In a mixing bowl, whisk your eggs, milk, salt and pepper. Add the eggs to the skillet and cook until just starting to set. Add in the bacon and sprinkle with cheese.
3. Cook until the egg is set and the cheese has melted, then flip over half of the omelette and cook for another minute. Serve and enjoy!

16. Greek Omelette

Enjoy the great flavours of this unique omelette. It is very filling!

Prep time: 10 minutes

Cook time: 8 minutes

Servings: 1

Ingredients:

- ¼ cup red onion, diced
- 2 tablespoons of milk
- 3 large eggs
- ½ cup grape tomatoes, halved
- ¼ cup feta cheese, crumbled
- 1 ½ cups baby spinach leafs, chopped
- 1 teaspoon olive oil
- sea salt (fine) & ground black pepper to taste

Directions:

1. Heat the oil in a nonstick skillet over medium heat. Add the spinach, and onion and sauté for about 5 minutes. Remove from the pan and set aside.

2. In a mixing bowl, whisk your eggs, milk, salt and pepper. Add to the pan and cook until starting to set, then add in the spinach mixture. Top with feta cheese and tomato, continue to cook until the egg is set. Flip half of the omelette over and cook for another minute. Serve and enjoy!

17. Ham & Cheese Omelette

A simple but tasty omelette recipe that makes for a great breakfast!

Prep time: 10 minutes

Cook time: 8 minutes

Servings: 1

Ingredients:

- 1 cup Swiss cheese, shredded
- 3 large eggs
- 2 tablespoons of milk
- 1 teaspoon olive oil
- 1 thick slice of cooked ham, chopped
- sea salt (fine) & ground black pepper as needed

Directions:

1. Heat your oil in a nonstick skillet over medium heat.
2. In a mixing bowl, whisk your eggs, milk, salt and pepper. Add the egg mixture to the skillet and cook until starting to set. Add in ham and top with cheese.
3. Continue to cook until the egg is set and the cheese is melted. Flip half of the omelette over and cook for another minute. Serve and enjoy!

18. Mexican Omelette

A fun twist on a traditional omelette that is so easy to make!

Prep time: 10 minutes

Cook time: 8 minutes

Servings: 1

Ingredients:

- ¼ cup red onion, diced
- 3 large eggs
- 2 tablespoons milk
- ½ cup salsa, drained
- ½ cup green bell pepper, chopped
- 1 cup Monterey Jack cheese, shredded
- sea salt (fine) & ground black pepper as needed
- 2 tablespoons butter

Directions:

1. Melt your butter in a nonstick skillet over medium heat. Add the onion and bell pepper, then sauté for about 5 minutes.

2. In a mixing bowl, whisk your eggs, milk, salt and pepper. Add the eggs to the pan and cook until set, then spoon salsa over eggs and top with cheese.

3. Cook until the egg is set and the cheese is melted, then flip half of the omelette over and cook for another minute. Serve and enjoy!

19. Brie & Herb Omelette

Enjoy this tasty mixture of simple ingredients that make for a savoury omelette!

Prep time: 10 minutes

Cook time: 8 minutes

Servings: 1

Ingredients:

- 2 tablespoons of milk
- 3 large eggs
- 2 slices of Brie cheese
- sea salt (fine) & ground black pepper to taste
- 1 teaspoon of olive oil
- 2 tablespoons parsley, chopped

Directions:

1. Heat your oil in a nonstick skillet over medium heat.
2. In a mixing bowl, whisk your eggs, milk, salt and pepper. Add the egg mixture to the skillet and cook until starting to set then place brie slices on top of the omelette.
3. Cook until the egg is set and then flip half of the omelette over and cook for another minute. Serve and enjoy!

20. Crab Omelette

A perfect omelette to serve on a special occasion or if you are having company over!

Prep time: 10 minutes

Cook time: 8 minutes

Servings: 1

Ingredients:

- 1 scallion, chopped
- 3 large eggs
- 2 tablespoons of milk
- ½ cup of crabmeat, flaked
- ½ cup Parmesan cheese, shredded
- sea salt (fine) & ground black pepper as needed
- 1 teaspoon olive oil

Directions:

1. Heat your oil in a nonstick skillet over medium heat.
2. In a mixing bowl, whisk your eggs, milk, salt and pepper. Add egg mixture to skillet and cook until almost set, then add crab and scallions. Top with cheese.
3. Cook until the egg is set, flip half of the omelette over and cook for another minute. Serve and enjoy!

21. Western Omelette

Savour this yummy recipe makes for a wonderful meal on a lazy weekend!

Prep time: 10 minutes

Cook time: 10 minutes

Servings: 2

Ingredients:

- 2 tablespoons milk
- ½ cup green bell pepper, chopped
- ¼ cup red onion, diced
- 4 large eggs
- ½ cup red bell pepper, chopped
- 2 tablespoons butter
- 4 thick slices of cooked ham, chopped
- 1 cup Monterey Jack cheese, shredded
- sea salt (fine) & ground black pepper as needed

Directions:

1. In a nonstick skillet, add your butter over medium heat. Add the bell peppers, and onion, and sauté for about 5 minutes. Add your chopped ham and cook for another minute.

2. In a mixing bowl, whisk your eggs, milk, salt and pepper.

3. Add the eggs to the skillet and cook until set, then add cheese.

4. Cook until the cheese has melted, flip half of the omelette over and continue to cook until set. Serve and enjoy!

22. Smoked Salmon & Green Onion Omelette

A lovely twist on a traditional omelette recipe—it makes for a great meal for a special breakfast lunch or brunch!

Prep time: 8 minutes

Cook time: 8 minutes

Servings: 1

Ingredients:

- 1 green onion, finely chopped
- 3 large eggs
- 2 tablespoons heavy cream
- ¼ cup smoked salmon, chopped
- ¼ cup cream cheese
- 1 teaspoon olive oil
- sea salt (fine) & ground black pepper

Directions:

1. In a nonstick skillet over medium heat, warm the oil.
2. In a mixing bowl, whisk your eggs, heavy cream, salt and pepper.
3. Add the eggs to the skillet and cook until set, then add salmon and green onions. Add the cream cheese over the top.
4. Cook until set, flip half of the omelette over and cook for another minute. Serve and enjoy!

23. Four Cheese Omelette

The cheese lovers will certainly love this yummy omelette recipe!

Prep time: 10 minutes

Cook time: 10 minutes

Servings: 1

Ingredients:

- 2 tablespoons of milk
- 3 large eggs
- ¼ cup Parmesan cheese
- ¼ cup Swiss cheese, shredded
- ¼ cup Cheddar cheese, shredded
- ¼ cup Emmenthal Cheese
- 1 scallion, chopped
- 1 tomato, chopped
- 1 teaspoon olive oil
- sea salt (fine) & ground black pepper

Directions:

1. Over medium heat warm your oil in a nonstick skillet.
2. In a mixing bowl, whisk the eggs with milk, salt and pepper.
3. Add to the skillet eggs, then cook until set, adding the scallions and tomato. Sprinkle the cheese over the top.
4. Cook until the cheese has melted, flip half the omelette over and cook for another minute. Serve and enjoy!

24. Spanish Omelette

A very filling omelette recipe that would make for a perfect dinner meal!

Prep time: 10 minutes

Cook time: 35 minutes

Servings: 3

Ingredients:

- 2 large potatoes, peeled & thinly sliced
- 8 large eggs
- 3 tablespoons of parsley, chopped
- 1 white onion, peeled & sliced
- 1 teaspoon olive oil
- sea salt (fine) & ground black pepper as needed

Directions:

1. In a skillet over medium heat, warm the oil. Add the potatoes and onion, then cook partially covered for 30 minutes.

2. In a mixing bowl, whisk your eggs, salt and pepper. Add eggs and parsley into skillet and cook until set.

3. Invert the omelette onto a plate, then add it back into the pan to cook on the other side for another minute. Serve and enjoy!

25. Artichoke & Goat Cheese Omelette

A great choice of omelette recipe to serve to your special guests!

Prep time: 10 minutes

Cook time: 8 minutes

Servings: 1

Ingredients:

- 3 marinated artichoke hearts, chopped
- 3 large eggs
- 2 tablespoons of milk
- ¼ cup goat cheese, crumbled
- ¼ cup red onion, diced
- 1 tablespoon olive oil
- sea salt (fine) & ground black pepper

Directions:

1. In a nonstick skillet over medium heat, warm your oil. Add onion and sauté for about 5 minutes. Add the artichokes and continue to cook for another minute or so then remove the pan from heat and set aside.

2. In a mixing bowl, whisk your eggs, milk, salt and pepper.

3. Add the eggs to the skillet and cook until starting to set. Add artichoke mixture and top with goat's cheese.

4. Continue to cook until the egg is set, then flip half of the omelette over and cook for another minute. Serve and enjoy! This is an omelette I often serve with garlic bread and a salad!

26. White Cheddar & Apple Smoked Bacon Omelette

Enjoy this easy-to-prepare omelette recipe that can be enjoyed in minutes!

Prep time: 8 minutes

Cook time: 8 minutes

Servings: 1

Ingredients:

- 1 cup white cheese, shredded
- 3 large eggs
- 2 tablespoons milk
- 2 slices of apple smoked bacon, cooked & crumbled
- 1 teaspoon olive oil
- sea salt (fine) & ground black pepper as needed

Directions:

1. Heat the oil over medium heat in a nonstick skillet.
2. In a mixing bowl, whisk your eggs, milk, salt and pepper. Add egg mixture to skillet and cook until set, then sprinkle with bacon and top with cheese.
3. Cook until the egg is set and the cheese is melted, then flip half of the omelette over and continue to cook for another minute. Serve and enjoy!

27. Pizza Omelette

A yummy omelette recipe that is sure to be popular with the kids!

Prep time: 8 minutes

Cook time: 8 minutes

Servings: 1

Ingredients:

- 8 slices of pepperoni
- 3 large eggs
- 2 tablespoons of milk
- ¼ cup pizza sauce
- ¼ cup mozzarella cheese, shredded
- 1 teaspoon olive oil
- sea salt (fine) & ground black pepperoni

Directions:

1. In a nonstick skillet warm the oil over medium heat.
2. In a mixing bowl, whisk your eggs together with milk, salt and pepper.
3. Add eggs to skillet and cook until set, then layer with pepperoni slices and top with cheese.
4. Cook for another minute or so or until the cheese is melted. Spread the pizza sauce over half of the omelette. Flip the other half of the omelette over and continue to cook for another minute. Serve and enjoy!

28. Mediterranean Omelette

Wonderful fresh Mediterranean savoury flavours all wrapped up in an omelette!

Prep time: 8 minutes

Cook time: 8 minutes

Servings: 1

Ingredients:

- 2 tablespoons of milk
- 3 large eggs
- 1 tablespoon of black olives, chopped
- ¼ cup feta cheese, crumbled
- 1 tablespoon of scallions, chopped
- 1 teaspoon olive oil
- sea salt (fine) & ground black pepper as needed
- ½ cup grape tomatoes, halved

Directions:

1. In a nonstick skillet over medium heat, warm the oil.
2. In a mixing bowl, combine olives, scallions, feta cheese, tomato, salt and pepper.
3. Add egg mixture to skillet and cook until set, then flip over half of the omelette and continue to cook for another minute. Serve and enjoy!

29. Shrimp Omelette

A great shrimp omelette recipe that makes for a quick and flavourful dinner!

Prep time: 10 minutes

Cook time: 8 minutes

Servings: 1

Ingredients:

- 8 medium-sized shrimp, peeled & deveined
- 3 large eggs
- 2 tablespoons of milk
- ½ cup green bell pepper, chopped
- ¼ cup red onion, diced
- ½ cup Monterey Jack cheese, shredded
- 2 tablespoons butter
- sea salt (fine) & fresh ground black pepper as needed

Directions:

1. In a nonstick skillet over medium heat, melt the butter. Add the bell pepper, onion and shrimp and sauté for about 4 minutes or until shrimp turn pink. Set in a bowl and set aside.

2. In a mixing bowl, whisk eggs, milk, salt and pepper.

3. Add egg mixture to skillet and layer the shrimp on top of starting to set eggs. Sprinkle top with cheese.

4. Cook until the cheese is melted, flip half of the omelette over and cook for another minute. Serve and enjoy!

30. Indian Omelette

A tasty and spicy omelette that is full of an abundance of flavour!

Prep time: 10 minutes

Cook time: 8 minutes

Servings: 1

Ingredients:

- 1 Serrano chile, minced
- 3 large eggs
- ¼ cup red onion, diced
- ¼ teaspoon paprika
- ¼ teaspoon turmeric powder
- 1 tablespoon fresh cilantro, finely chopped
- 1 tablespoon olive oil
- sea salt & fresh ground black pepper

Directions:

1. Heat the oil in a nonstick skillet over medium heat.
2. In a mixing bowl, whisk eggs along with the rest of the ingredients until well combined.
3. Add to skillet and cook until eggs are set. Flip the omelette completely over then continue to brown for about 2 minutes. Serve and enjoy!

Conclusion

I am extending my sincere thanks to you for choosing to purchase my omelette recipe cookbook. I truly hope you and your loved ones will continue to use this collection of omelette recipes like my loved ones and I have for many years! I encourage you to truly make the recipe your own by trying to add new ingredients to the base recipes. You can express your tastes and preferences by adding ingredients that please your tastes! Also, I would encourage you to get loved ones involved in the preparation process of your meal. A great way to strengthen bonds with loved ones is to make time to prepare and share a meal! Time is precious, especially in this fast-paced world we live in today—it is essential to "make time" for those special times!

Afterword

Readers like you are the reason I get up in the morning. I am delighted that you decided to download and read my Books.

I can't thank you enough for choosing healthy living via your choice to engage in healthy and creative cooking. It means a lot to me because I poured my heart and passion into every page of this cookbook. And this is why I hope that you'd get absolute fulfillment from reading and exploring cooking with this recipe book.

I know that there are lots of similar culinary content like this everywhere, but it gives me joy that you chose mine. Hence, I'd appreciate it if you could help with your thoughts about this book. Feedback from customers helps me do better, so I don't mind getting a few from you.

You can do that by leaving a review on Amazon.com.

Thanks!

Olivia Rana

Printed in Great Britain
by Amazon